IMPROVE YOUR MOOD IN *MINUTES!*

No matter who we are or what we do, achieving happiness is our ultimate goal. Work, food, sex, entertainment, children—the underlying reason for most of our actions is to guarantee some degree of lifelong pleasure. But why, then, are there so few of us who consider ourselves happy?

A successful advertising whiz kid, Siimon Reynolds had it all—money, fame, power, looks, love—but he still wasn't happy, and he was determined to find out why. He tried therapy and meditation, read every expert from Confucius to Deepak Chopra, but couldn't find the key to the basic everyday cheerfulness he craved. Then he turned to science—and found his answers.

Let Siimon Reynolds share those answers with you.

BECOME HAPPY IN EIGHT MINUTES

Siimon Reynolds, age 31, has already built and sold three advertising agencies in New York and Sydney, Australia, and won numerous awards for his campaigns in the United States, the United Kingdom, and Australia. Currently the executive director of the John Singleton Agency in Sydney, he is also a popular inspirational speaker on the subject of personal and professional success.

Become Happy
in
Eight Minutes

Siimon Reynolds

A PLUME BOOK

PLUME
Published by the Penguin Group
Penguin Books USA Inc., 375 Hudson Street,
New York, New York 10014, U.S.A.
Penguin Books Ltd, 27 Wrights Lane,
London W8 5TZ, England
Penguin Books Australia Ltd, Ringwood, Victoria, Australia
Penguin Books Canada Ltd, 10 Alcorn Avenue,
Toronto, Ontario, Canada M4V 3B2
Penguin Books (N.Z.) Ltd, 182–190 Wairau Road,
Auckland 10, New Zealand

Penguin Books Ltd, Registered Offices:
Harmondsworth, Middlesex, England

Published by Plume, an imprint of Dutton Signet,
a division of Penguin Books USA Inc.

ISBN 0-452-27488-5

Printed in the United States of America
Set in Century Light

CONTENTS

The Search
for Happiness

Everybody is searching for happiness.

No matter what your age, no matter what your occupation, it is in your nature to get up every morning and do things that you believe will make you happier. Happiness is the goal of goals, the Holy Grail of most people's existence. Ask people in the street for the one wish they'd like granted, and most wouldn't be clamoring to be a movie star or have a million dollars in the bank; the majority would simply reply, "I just want to be happy."

Yet hardly any of us are. Indeed, after an exhaustive worldwide research study, the renowned happiness psychologist, Mihaly Csikszentmihalyi, concluded, "Genuinely happy individuals are few and far between."

Perhaps one of the reasons we're not happy is that many of us think happiness is an impossible

> How to gain, how to keep, how to
> recover happiness is in fact for
> most people at all times the secret
> motive of all they do.
>
> —WILLIAM JAMES, philosopher

goal, achieved only by shaven-headed monks after decades of training in remote monasteries in northern Tibet.

Nothing could be further from the truth. Biologists and behavioral scientists working in cooperation have learned what creates good and bad moods in human beings. By painstakingly analyzing how the brain works, they've put together numerous ways of improving your mood in minutes. (Yes, minutes.) But while this data has been published in scientific reports and psychiatric periodicals, never before has this information appeared in one short, sharp, easy-to-understand book.

Become Happy in Eight Minutes will teach you exactly that. It won't teach you the truth about God, our place in the cosmos, or how to be blissed out twenty-four hours a day, seven days a week. But it *will* clearly explain how to get into a happier mood than you are in now. Quickly.

If you're feeling terrible, you'll be able to feel better fast. If you're already feeling okay, these techniques will get you feeling happy and contented in far less time than it takes to fill a presciption for Prozac.

> We all want to be happy, and we're all going to die. . . . You might say those are the only two unchallengeably true facts that apply to every human being on this planet.
>
> —WILLIAM BOYD, writer

We all get in terrible moods, let's face it. But it doesn't mean you have to *stay* in a bad mood. Put the techniques of this book into practice, and you'll be able to change your mood in moments. Become adept at these methods, and people around you will quickly notice how "up" you seem to be. You will shortly experience the kind of happy feelings that elude the majority of people for most of their lives.

The impact on your life will be extraordinary if you put this technique into practice with all your heart. Why? Because every area of your life is deeply affected by your moods. If you can stay in a good mood at the office, then obviously you're going to work more effectively. You'll spend less time bickering with that nagging Attila the Hun boss and more time scoring pay-dirt deals.

If you're in a good mood at home, you'll get on better with your family. People like being around people who are happy, so when you improve your moods, the quantity and the quality of your friends will improve too. Even your dog will notice the difference if you're happier—more walks, less yelling!

The ability to get yourself out of bad moods fast will work wonders on the quality of your life, and

▼

Happiness is having a large, loving, caring, close-knit family, in another city.

—GEORGE BURNS, comedian

▲

probably on its length. Ask any expert in the burgeoning field of psychoimmunology. The happier you are, the more you're likely to have an immune system strong enough to ward off disease. Even the quality of our cells is affected by our moods.

You may think it sounds just too good to be true. How, you ask, can something that seems so difficult be achieved so easily and quickly? Well, thank science. Once it seemed impossible that man could fly, yet now we cross the globe in less than a day as we sit back, munch on peanuts, and quaff champagne. Once the thought of having more light than candlepower could provide seemed a pipe dream; yet these days the flick of a switch can light up an entire football field. Where once messages took weeks to travel a hundred miles, now they can go to the planet Mars in minutes. All because scientists unlocked secrets not previously understood by mankind.

If such major advances were made by science in the world around us, doesn't it make sense that science has made great leaps in knowledge *within* us? Of course it does, and in the following pages I will present some of those important new jewels of information.

Eventually, the ideas in this book (all the techniques are proven by research, remember) will be known and utilized by everyone. It won't be considered unusual at all. In fact, in the future anybody *not* utilizing these techniques may well be considered primitive! But for now these simple methods will be known only to a few—the science world's pioneers and people who read this book.

How did I find out about these breakthroughs in human technology? Allow me to give you a brief background to my research.

I was once one of those so-called "whiz kids" of

> The U.S. Constitution doesn't guarantee happiness, only the pursuit of it. You have to catch up with it yourself.
>
> —BENJAMIN FRANKLIN, statesman-philosopher

business. By my mid-twenties I had cofounded an incredibly successful advertising agency in Australia and also set up one of the hottest young agencies in New York (according to the *New York Times*). Within a year of starting operations, we boasted both Toyota and Philip Morris as clients. I was on TV shows, I was invited to all the "cool" parties, I even won a "Young Achievers" award for career achievement, but something was missing.

I spent all my time striving but never arriving. I was so committed to getting more *things*, that I hadn't devoted any time to my internal wealth. In short, I wasn't happy. Thankfully, though, from a very young age my parents had instilled in me the value of learning. So, faced with a painful awareness of deep inner dissatisfaction, I decided once and for all to get to the bottom of the "happiness thing."

I devoured book after book after book, reading until the early hours of the morning, searching for something, anything, that could reveal knowledge and get me closer to being happy.

Along the way I found out some fascinating stuff about the art and science of happiness. I read the work of Norman Cousins, who in *Anatomy of an Illness* wrote how he beat a terminal disease by teaching himself how to laugh and really enjoy life.

I read the works of Deepak Chopra, a brilliant man educated in both western medicine and ancient Indian Ayurvedic healing techniques. This modern-day guru presented research study after research study proving that your happiness directly affects your health.

I studied countless books from the medical fraternity, from Dr. Maxwell Maltz to Dr. Spencer Johnson. I scoured bookstores to learn what philosophers had to say about happiness, immersing myself in the ancient texts of Lao-tzu, Confucius, and Da Mo and the modern ones of Daisetz Suzuki, Jon Winokur, Paramahansa Yogananda, John Blofeld, Mantak Chia, and myriad others. (See page 117 for "The Happiness Library.")

I learned a lot. But I also learned that knowing things is not enough. Unless you make them a part of your life, really use them and test them and rigorously refine them, they won't have any effect on you. So I put what I'd learned into practice, with some stunning results. I immediately tripled my happy moods and dramatically reduced my down periods. It was a real breakthrough in my search for happiness. At last I felt more *control* over my life and my moods.

> Too much of a good thing can
> be wonderful.
>
> —MAE WEST, actress

The funny thing was, it wasn't long at all before the people around me noticed the difference too. Friends and work associates began to inquire how I managed to be "up" so often, how I could be so emotionally strong and stable. The merest expression of interest was enough to start me pontificating on all the great scientific stuff I'd learned about mood control and the colossal difference it had made in my life. People were so transfixed by my discoveries that I decided to share them. And so this book was born.

Here, in a nutshell, is what you'll learn in *Become Happy in Eight Minutes*:

In "Minute One," I'll introduce you to a tiny but powerful part of your body: the thymus gland. This gland may seem small and insignificant, but it actually plays a starring role in creating your moods. It can be stimulated quickly and easily whenever you need to pep up your spirits, with the three simple exercises that I outline.

In "Minutes Two and Three," we'll be investigating the impact your breathing has on your happiness. Believe it or not, how you breathe plays a major part in the mood you're in. If you breathe the

> ▼
>
> There is no duty we so much
> underrate as the duty of
> being happy.
>
> —ROBERT LOUIS STEVENSON, writer
>
> ▲

right way, it's nearly impossible to stay unhappy. Likewise, if you breathe in the wrong way, melancholic moods will be your constant companion.

Ever notice how you sometimes feel much better after a good meal? Well, that's because what you eat and drink directly affects your mind's chemical balance and, therefore, your moods. We'll be looking into the power of food and drink on your brain during "Minute Four." I'll show you how just drinking a glass of fruit juice begins a process that can have you feeling on top of the world.

The second half of the process is outlined in "Minutes Five and Six." Here I explain how you can utilize the startling power of the brain to effect a huge increase in your happiness, energy, and overall well-being. By the end of this chapter, you'll better understand why you've achieved the results you have in your life and how you can break through your success and happiness barriers to help you live the life you always knew was possible.

Your body movements are also crucial to how good or bad you feel. In "Minute Seven," I'll show you exactly how to hold and move your body to improve your mood radically. This technique *alone*, used consistently, can have a profoundly positive effect on the quality of your life.

In "Minute Eight," I'll prove to you that many of the bad moods we have are a result of what we focus on. If you're always brooding over the negative things in your life, a bitter existence is assured. However, if you regularly practice the simple focus-controlling techniques I describe, your brain has almost no choice but to be happy. Believe me, these techniques work.

In the next chapter I look into what creates long-term life happiness. What are the personality characteristics (there are eight) of truly happy people and, more important, how can you develop

> Happiness is a condition that must be prepared for, cultivated and defended privately by each person.
>
> —MIHALYI CSIKSZENTMIHALYI, psychologist

them? A life overflowing with happiness is not a matter of luck. I'll show you a series of daily practices that will dramatically increase your levels of bliss for the rest of your life.

Finally, I conclude by talking about the books on happiness that have radically changed my life. The search for true happiness is a lifelong journey, and the books I outline in the last chapter will be of great assistance to you as you travel along this golden path.

Don't worry if you flunked science at school; every technique in this book is simple. You don't need to be a mixture of Einstein, Pythagoras, and Newton to comprehend it; all you need is a willing-

▼

It is neither wealth nor splendor,
but tranquillity and occupation
which give happiness.

—THOMAS JEFFERSON, statesman-
philosopher

▲

ness to learn and practice the techniques, a little
faith in yourself and your hidden abilities, and, most
of all, an open mind. Without a mind open enough
to accept unusual concepts, no great learning will
ever be achieved.

Consider the story of a brash young student of
Zen philosophy who went to visit a wise old master
up in the mountains. The student asked the master
to tell him all the secrets he knew about life. As
soon as the benevolent teacher began talking, the
student interrupted. Then hardly a minute went by
without the youngster disagreeing with or question-
ing the master's knowledge.

Exasperated, the master stopped teaching and instead asked the student if he'd like a cup of tea. The student agreed. The master poured some tea for his visitor into a cup but kept pouring and pouring until the tea overflowed out of the cup, all over the table and onto the floor. Eventually the student could stand it no longer. "Stop! Stop!" he exclaimed. "Can't you see the cup is full? No more will go in!" "Your mind is like the cup," said the master. "Unless you empty it of all your opinions, how can you allow any new knowledge to fit in?"

So keep an open mind and enjoy the book. It will take you only an hour or so to read. But it may well change your life.

▼

Minute One:

Stimulate the Thymus Gland

▲

▶ **T**here is excellent scientific evidence to suggest that stimulation of the body's thymus gland will result in greater feelings of pleasure and happiness. This is because when the thymus gland* is activated, it changes the chemicals in the body to a mix that soothes the body's nervous system and enhances the brain's functioning. Hence, a feeling of increased comfort comes over you.

For years doctors didn't understand the vitally important role played by the thymus gland in our body. As late as 1960, the function of the thymus was competely unknown. Some of the more remarkable breakthroughs came from mind-body

---

* There are many hundreds of glands throughout the body. Their purpose is to secrete substances either internally or externally. (Glands that produce an internal secretion are known as endocrine glands.)

> To be truly happy, be indifferent
> to life's ups and downs.
>
> —TAKIO SAITO, karate master

specialist Dr. John Diamond and his team. In his seminal text *Your Body Doesn't Lie*, Dr. Diamond presents a study indicating that this powerful gland acts as the chief executive of the body's healing energies, controlling them to a large extent.

The impact our thymus gland has on us is illustrated by Dr. Diamond's tests on another warm-blooded creature—the common rat. He discovered that if you remove the thymus of a rat, the creature becomes powerless to overcome any cancer cells that are injected into it. Leave the thymus gland in the rodent, however, and, Dr. Diamond found, the rat statistically has a far greater chance of overcoming the cancerous cells and living a long, healthy life. Many experts, like the great cancer researcher and Australian Nobel Prize–winner Sir Macfarlane Burnet, believe that stimulating the thymus gland's activity will result in strengthening the human body's ability to protect itself from cancer.

Why haven't we all heard about this before, you ask? It's because this complex data usually gets published in medical journals and never makes it to mainstream publications. There is so much information being published on cancer and health that much of it just gets lost in the labyrinthine medical research system. While the thymus may be discussed frequently by medical scholars and researchers, they either don't want to or can't get the public to take notice of it. But stimulation of the thymus really can make a difference to a person's happiness, as we shall see.

One of the primary reasons the thymus is so beneficial to our well-being is that it produces "T cells." What's so special about T cells? Well, any doctor worth the letters "M.D." after his or her name will tell you that T cells are the body's super police. They're always on the beat, looking out for abnormal cells—cells that can do the body harm. Once the T cells spot a danger, they act like the

▼

Talk happiness. The world
is sad enough
Without your woe. No
path is wholly rough.

—ELLA WHEELER WILCOX,
poet and journalist

▲

Terminator and quickly destroy it. So you really owe
a lot to those little Ts wandering around your body.

Okay, you think, if my thymus gland is so important, tell me where it is. It's not that hard to find.
In fact, it's just behind the upper part of the breastbone in the middle of your chest. Now, how do you
stimulate your thymus? There are three simple
methods.

The first technique of thymus stimulation is to
smile! That's it, just smile. Every time you smile,
your thymus gland is activated; every time it's ac-

tivated, it sends a small wave of chemicals through your body, making you feel subtly better. Remarkable, but absolutely true.

The ability of a simple smile to create a happy feeling inside the body has been extremely well documented in a 1993 University of California study, led by Dr. Paul Ekman. The study found that smiling activates the thymus and also muscles connected to various pleasure centers in the human brain, creating the effect of "spontaneous enjoyment." The interesting thing is that it isn't just any old smile that sets the pleasure center's bells ringing. Only one type of smile can do it. It's known as

Happiness is a perfume. You cannot pour it on others without getting a few drops on yourself.

—ANONYMOUS

The happiness of a man
in this life does not consist in
the absence but in the mastery
of the passions.

—ALFRED LORD TENNYSON, poet

the Duchenne smile, after the nineteenth-century French neurologist who first investigated facial muscles.

According to Dr. Ekman, "The key markers of the Duchenne smile that readily distinguish it from all others are the crow's-feet wrinkles around the eyes and a subtle drop in the eye cover fold so that the skin about the eye moves down slightly toward the eyeball." In other words, a half-hearted grin won't help much in changing your feelings; it has to be a full-blooded, big, broad, sincere smile.

The next step in thymus stimulation is manual stimulation of the thymus. You do this simply by placing two fingers on top of the gland (see illustration on page 29) and tapping solidly about twenty times. Keep smiling throughout.

The final easy step to thymus invigoration involves your tongue. All you do is place your tongue behind your upper teeth on the roof of your mouth. You may be starting to feel a bit silly, but Dr. Diamond and his researchers have found that by simply placing your tongue in this "centering" position, your two brain hemispheres become more balanced, helping you think better and feel better. (Diamond is the first Westerner to appreciate the benefits of placing the tongue in the centering position, but as early as 1,000 B.C. Chinese Chi Kung meditation experts were practicing the same technique.)

Actually, it's a good idea to place your tongue in this position all through the day, whenever it occurs to you. It may feel a bit strange at first, but you'll be pleasantly surprised at the soothing effect this brain-centering position has on your moods.

Let's put these ideas to the test right now. Sit somewhere comfortable, away from noise and distractions. Relax your muscles and smile. Smile as if

One is happy as a result of one's
own efforts, once one knows of
the necessary ingredients of
happiness—simple tastes, a certain
degree of courage, self-denial to a
point, love of work, and, above all,
a clear conscience. Happiness is no
vague dream, of that I now
feel certain.

—GEORGE SAND, writer

you are the happiest person in the world. Smile as
though you haven't got a care in the universe. The
second you do this, your thymus gland will move
into action and begin to stimulate the body in its
very positive way. Do the thymus tap twenty times
and keep your tongue in the centering position for
at least one minute.

Illustration by Lauren R. Lyde

By the way, while you're smiling you should always relax your eyes, as they play a vital part in your moods. Each eye is linked to the metonymic nervous system, a vital regulator of your body's organs and glands. When something happens to you,

O happiness! our being's
    end and aim!
Good, pleasure, ease,
    content! whate'er thy name:
That something still which
    prompts th'eternal sigh,
For which we bear to live,
    or dare to die.

—ALEXANDER POPE, poet

your eyes are normally the first to receive the emotional signals, and they then cause the body's organs and glands to change their functioning in response. So when you're smiling, simply relax your eyes and your whole body will relax too.

Please don't expect your body to go into a euphoric state of bliss the second you grin like a Cheshire cat; it doesn't work like that. But know that as you smile and stimulate your thymus, the chemical structure of your body is being changed for the better and mild natural relaxants are being sent through it, which will gradually begin to lighten your mood.

All this, and we're only at Minute One. Let's move ahead!

Minutes Two and Three:

Change Your Breathing

Who could doubt the importance of breath to our lives? We can survive for weeks without food, days without water, but only minutes without breathing. (And a very unpleasant few minutes they would be!)

Without breath we are nothing, but how many of us actually think about our breathing? Precious few. Yet scientists know that improving our breathing will improve our health.

Here's how it works:

We all know we've got blood pumping through our bodies, but most of us don't realize there is another fluid that also travels around in our system. In fact, there is four times as much of this stuff as there is blood.

Happiness is the sublime moment
when you get out of your corsets
at night.

—JOYCE GRENFELL, actress

Doctors call this substance *lymph*.* Lymph sur-
rounds each and every cell in your body, and you've
got billions of those. Lymph is the body's janitor. It
gets rid of all the dirty goo and gunk that ends up
in your system during everyday life—anything toxic
and anything dead (like dead blood cells). Healthy
lymph is absolutely crucial to a healthy body. Otherwise, all that toxic stuff builds up, and pretty soon
it's "Goodbye, world!"

Everybody knows how blood circulates; the
heart pumps it. But how does lymph circulate?

* For the technically minded, lymph is a colorless fluid de-
rived from the blood and circulates in the lymphatic vessels in
the body.

The only ways are muscular movement (hence the value of exercise) and deep breathing. Without good, strong, deep breathing your immune system may well become very weak indeed. Deep breathing also massages your internal organs and glands, and stimulates your hormone secretions.

Breathing doesn't affect just your physical health; it dramatically affects your mood as well. Think about it. When you're watching a horror movie and you're scared, what happens? Your breathing gets slow and shallow. You may be too busy worrying about the One-Eyed Green Monster from the Black Lagoon to notice your breathing change, but it does. When you're excited in a positive way, your breathing is a bit different. It's short but a little deeper, and you tend to take in more oxygen.

When you're calm and blissfully content and happy, your style of breathing changes yet again. Pay attention next time you're in this state, and you'll see that your breath is long and deep and as regular as clockwork. This kind of breath is the optimum.

What works one way also works the other.

> God designed us to be happy,
> but gave us the choice.
>
> —ANDERS RIVE, sculptor

If your moods change your breathing, then it makes sense that your breathing changes your moods.

It's a proven scientific fact; alter your breath pattern and you'll alter your mood. Any brain physiologist will tell you that it's true. So will any yogi.* In over 3,000 years of study and training, the Indian and Chinese yogis have become experts on the effects of breathing on the mind.

One of India's greatest living yogis, B. K. S. Iyen-

---

* A yogi is one who is dedicated to the cultivation of the higher aspects of mind and body. There are a wide variety of styles of yoga ranging from Hatha, which consists mainly of physical exercises, to Raja, which is more spiritual in nature. You may think of yogis as "those guys who levitate and sleep on beds of nails."

gar, had this to say on the subject: "The yogi's life is not measured by the number of his days but by the number of his breaths. Therefore, he follows the proper rhythmic pattern of slow, deep breathing. These rhythmic patterns strengthen the respiratory system, soothe the nervous system, and reduce craving."

You may think the idea that our lives are based on our number of breaths is a loony concept, but there is some evidence to support it. For example, animals that are famous for living a long time—like the elephant, tortoise, or snake—all breathe very slowly. The giant tortoise, which has been known to live over 300 years, breathes just four times a minute.

As far back as the seventeenth century, there were people who understood how breathing changes people's moods. At about that time, the legendary mystic Karila wrote the following:

> If you want to have a calm spirit, first regulate your breathing. For when that is under control, the heart will be at peace. But when breathing is spasmodic, then it will be troubled. Therefore, before attempting anything, first regulate your breathing, and your spirit will be calmed.

> No man chooses evil because it is
> evil; he only mistakes it for
> happiness, the good he seeks.
>
> —MARY WOLLSTONECRAFT SHELLEY, writer

Changing your breathing can make an extraordinary difference on how good your mood is. The trouble is, hardly anyone breathes properly. Many people only use a third of their lungs when they breathe. The key is to use your diaphragm, not just your chest. Breathing like this may seem unnatural to you, but it's actually how we were meant to breathe. Look at a dog or cat asleep. They breathe with deep abdominal breaths, not shallow chest breaths. Next time you're at a zoo, check out other animals too. You'll find that all other creatures breathe using their abdomen. It's only we humans who, through a mixture of ignorance and laziness, have degenerated into chest breathers.

If you breathe only with your chest, you must take about three times as many breaths to get the same amount of air as a deep abdominal breath would give you. If each abdominal breath gives you about three times more oxygen, imagine what a difference breathing that way can make to your health over a lifetime.

So don't just sit there; why not try a few correct deep breaths and see how they affect your mood?

Here's a simple technique for breathing correctly.

First, get comfortable and relax. Now take a deep breath. Instead of just filling up your chest, fill the bottom of your lungs with air first. You do this by pushing the stomach softly out as you inhale through your nose. Once you've filled the bottom half of your lungs, continue inhaling and fill the top half, around the chest. Be sure to fill both parts of your lungs in one smooth inhalation. Hold the breath for a couple of seconds; then slowly exhale through your nose in a calm, relaxed manner. Don't take so much air in that you feel like bursting.

> Happiness lies in good health and
> a bad memory.
>
> —INGRID BERGMAN, actress

Do this for two minutes with your eyes closed, while you maintain the gentle smile from Step One. Breathe as if you're blissfully happy. Go on, try it now . . . How do you feel? I know you've begun to feel happier; your deep breaths are replenishing your system and slowing down the speed of your thoughts. You'll be starting to think more clearly as your brain is affected by the increase in oxygen flowing through.

You've just completed the second step to mood changing, and the most powerful steps are yet to come. . . .

▼

Minute Four:

Drink
Fruit Juice

▲

Now we're moving into high gear. We're going to dramatically change how you feel inside, and we're going to do it in just a few short minutes—not with the aid of some sophisticated scientific gizmo, but with a humble glass of fruit juice. Yes, fruit juice.

Do you know someone who always seems to be cranky? Who always seems to have gotten up on the wrong side of the bed? Well, don't be too hard on them. It may not be their personality; it may well be their diet.

What you eat drastically affects your moods. If you eat foods that are low on nourishment and high on fat, you're just asking for a shortage of energy and therefore a low mood. A lack of energy tells you that your brain is undersupplied with fuel, which leads to impaired thinking abilities. That's why "Type A" personalities who eat fast food and skip breakfast to save time find after a few years they've burnt out. No longer are their minds as quick and efficient as steel traps, nor can they concentrate for long periods of time.

Not only does your food intake affect your mental abilities; it of course profoundly affects your physical well-being too. For instance, tests in a number of U.S. prisons have shown that when the inmates eat more salads and less junk food, the violence rate inside the prison drops significantly. (It is no coincidence that most hard-core criminals have not been raised on healthy diets.)

Youth is happy because it has the capacity to see Beauty. Anyone who keeps the ability to see Beauty never grows old.

—FRANZ KAFKA, writer

Buddhist monks are almost always vegetarians. Their research has shown that when they don't eat meat, they have calmer emotions, more conducive to meditation.

Western dietitians reach similar conclusions, and even to the laymen it makes sense. Just as different quality gasoline affects a car's performance, so too our vehicle (the body) is affected by the poor fuel we put inside us. Can you imagine putting cheap gas in a Formula One racing car? Hardly. Mechanics know that without premium-grade fuel, high performance is simply an impossibility.

There are foods that fill you with energy and others that use up energy. Some are good for the mind, and some are good for the heart. Many are good for nothing at all. There are millions of books on the subject of diet (many with completely opposing opinions), but two I urge you to look at are *Perfect Health* by Deepak Chopra and *Diet for a New America* by John Robbins. Chopra's book tells you how to fit your diet to your body's needs, while Robbins tells you the hard truth about what's really in your food.

I don't intend to go into all the variables of diet,

> The happiest women, like the
> happiest nations, have no history.
>
> —GEORGE ELIOT, writer

but I do want to take a moment to discuss the
connection between fruit juice and the mind. The
"pick-me-up" effect that comes from drinking pure
(and I stress pure) fruit juice is due to the quick
rise in blood-sugar levels it creates. Fruit juice* is
jam-packed with a kind of sugar called glucose.
What's so special about glucose? It's the prime fuel
that the brain burns for energy. When you take in
a lot of glucose, your brain is bursting with get-up-

---

* Fruit juice is a great source of nutrients. It's high in fiber
and packed with antioxidants (nutrients that are proven to
slow the aging process). But be careful about the juice you buy.
Many so-called "fruit-juice drinks" contain less than 20 percent
real fruit juice, the rest usually being water and sugar. Fresh
is best—indeed, there is a widely held theory among naturo-
paths that even freshly squeezed fruit juice that is more than
a few hours old has lost much of its "life force" and nutrients.

and-go, making you feel a whole lot better than you did before.

Couldn't you just consume anything sugary? Why does it have to be juice? Well, most sugary foods will eventually increase your energy, but often they will take a lot more time to do so. Because many fruit juices are acidic, they pass through the stomach and arrive at the small intestine, ready for use, very quickly.

Also, many sugary foods are absolutely terrible for you. Some are just a bunch of chemicals in a brightly colored wrapper. (In fact, I believe that in the future people will look back at our time and be incredulous that some of the foods we ate were even legal.) Pure, fresh fruit juice, though, is excellent for your health.

Now for the bad news.

Unfortunately, the sugar high doesn't last forever. In fact, after about half an hour of feeling "up," the effect will begin to diminish, and after an hour and a half it will be virtually as if you had never gulped it down at all.

So what's the point in swallowing the juice if the effect is going to wear off soon afterward? Well, it

> 'Tis only happiness can keep
> us young.
>
> —MAGA, philosopher

all depends on what you do during that half-hour "up" period. And believe me, you're going to be doing a lot.

Think of a glider soaring high in the sky. There's only one way to get a glider up that high. They use an airplane to take it up there, unhook the towing cable, and away it goes.

Think of yourself as the glider and the fruit juice as the airplane that gets you up there. But how do you keep on flying? You stay up by making sure that while you're under the beneficial influence of the juice, you alter the way you are thinking. While you're temporarily feeling good, you can start improving your thinking (making it more positive and powerful); then, by the time the juice wears off, you'll have gotten out of your bad mood and into a good one.

When you're feeling really lousy, you need the aid of a powerful mental stimulant to get yourself into that good mood. You're like a glider who needs a plane to help it up into the clear blue sky. Fortunately, as you're about to learn, science has discovered some great ways to get you into a good mood quickly once you've swallowed your juice.

In fact, master the following methods and they will not only change your mood, but they can also help you alter almost any aspect of your life that makes you unhappy.

Minutes Five and Six:

Reprogram Your Brain

▶ **I**n the United States lives a man by the name of Seymour Cray. Cray is the creator of one of the most powerful computers in the world, the Cray supercomputer. If the Cray supercomputer goes all out, it can do well over 400 million calculations every second. *Every second!*

But get this: If the Cray supercomputer works full speed for *100 years*, it can only do what your brain can do in *one minute.* You are in possession of the world's most powerful computer. It's sitting inside your head! Yet, incredibly, you hardly use it. According to renowned brain expert Tony Buzan, the most modern research indicates we use only about *one percent* of our brainpower. Embarrassing but true.

Now imagine if we accepted that kind of failure rate in other areas of our lives. If surgeons only got

> Seek happiness in the present, and you'll find it in the future.
>
> —Kazuo Suzuki, karate master

it right one percent of the time, there'd sure be a lot of unhappy people around. What if architects only got one percent of houses right? We'd all be wearing construction helmets twenty-four hours a day! No, we'd never accept that performance level in any other area of our life. Yet with our own brain, the very thing that *creates our entire future*, we put up with this abysmal performance.

The good news is that in the next few pages I'm going to show you how to use more of your brain's power.

The first step to using more of your brain is getting to know a bit about how the old gray matter works.

To put it simply, your mind is split into two sections: the subconscious and the conscious. The conscious mind does all of your rational thinking (like deciding whether you should eat that extra jelly doughnut, or how to get to Tom's house the quickest way). That's the part of the brain most of us are aware of.

But what most of us *don't* know is that the greater part—in fact *88 percent*—of the brain is subconscious. And boy, is it an incredible instrument. For instance, your heartbeat, your digestion, indeed every one of the billions of physical processes happening in your body every second, is looked after by your subconscious mind. You don't even have to "think" about it: your subconscious handles it all.

Happiness: a good bank account, a good cook, and a good digestion.

—JEAN-JACQUES ROUSSEAU, philosopher

But your subconscious doesn't rule just your body; it's the power station of your mind too. In fact, you are what you are and where you are in life as a result of what's in your subconscious.

You see, the subconscious mind acts like a huge memory sponge. Everything that has ever happened to you in your life is perfectly recorded inside it. (The fact that you don't seem to remember it all is irrelevant.) That's pretty amazing. But what's even more amazing is that neuroscientists have discovered that your subconscious mind has no mechanism for recognizing what is real and what is not real. Instead, it just accepts all the information you give it as being correct!

So let's just think about all this for a moment. If the brain controls our actions, thoughts, and performance; and if the subconscious is 88 percent of the brain; and if it can't tell the difference between what's true or false but just acts on whatever information you give it, then that means just one thing:

You can program your brain to make you do and feel virtually whatever you want.

Let me give you just one example of the scientific proof of this theory. A few years ago the science journal *Research Quarterly* reported that a group of scientists had gotten three groups of students to practice basketball free throws. The first group were told to physically practice throwing the ball through the hoop (from a preset distance) for twenty days. The second group weren't to practice at all; and the third group were to practice mentally only—to just *imagine* that they were getting the ball in the hoop, again and again and again.

The results were staggering. The first group, who practiced physically, improved 24 percent after the twenty-day period. Not bad. The second group, who didn't practice at all, showed no improvement whatsoever. (No surprises there.) But the third group, who only practiced mentally, improved *23 percent*! They improved almost as much as the first group, *yet they never even picked up a ball*.

Why? Because they just told their subconscious they were great basketball players! The subconscious couldn't tell that they were just visualizing playing well; it thought they were actually playing! After a while the brain "learned" that the students were great basketball players, and it directed their bodies to continue playing at that level.

> That is happiness; to be dissolved
> into something complete and great.
>
> —WILLA CATHER, writer

As Dr. John C. Eccles and Sir Charles Sherrinton, the eminent brain physiologists, put it, "When you learn anything, a pattern of neurons forming a chain is set up in your brain tissue. This chain, or electrical pattern, is your brain's method of remembering. So, since the subconscious cannot distinguish a real from an imagined experience, perfect mental practice can change, or correct, imperfect electrical patterns grooved there."

As a result of these and other similar findings, there now isn't an Olympic team that doesn't spend countless hours on mental training of the subconscious mind. In some cases, as athletes near their event, fully 50 percent of their training is mental rehearsal of the race.

Mental reprogramming works whether you want to achieve a major goal or just change your mood from sad to happy. It's easy to get your brain to help improve your mood. I'll show you how right now. Get your body relaxed once again. Continue your smile and your deep breaths, and trust that the fruit juice you drank is already quietly picking up your mood.

Close your eyes.

Now pretend you're at the movies, but this time the screen is in your head. With your eyes still closed, see yourself on that movie screen. See yourself as happy as you've ever been. See yourself jumping for joy, smiling, laughing, playing, in total

What is happiness? The feeling that power *increases*—that resistance is being overcome.

—FRIEDRICH NIETZSCHE, philosopher

bliss. See that picture of yourself without a care in the world, free as a bird, delirious with happiness.

Really concentrate on making that picture feel like a reality. Make the picture on the screen as clear and as big as possible. Make the movie super-colorful, and nice and loud. (You may even like to imagine that your favorite upbeat song is playing as well in the background.) When you've got that picture as happy as you want it, keep visualizing it for at least two full minutes. It's very important you do it with as much commitment, conviction, and intensity as possible.

And that's it. That's all it takes to begin to give your subconscious mind new instructions. The two keys are to *really emotionally feel that the picture on the screen is actually happening* and to *repeat the picture again and again.* When you do this *intensely* for a couple of minutes, your brain will begin to direct you to follow your visualization, and you will soon be feeling happier, stronger, more carefree. So use this technique any time you're feeling down. The more you use it, the stronger your visualization skills will get.

Remember that your brain is just a computer.

> Man is the artificer of his
> own happiness.
>
> —HENRY DAVID THOREAU, writer

The reason you're feeling down is because *you* instructed your brain to feel down. It wasn't necessarily a bad event or a bad person that made you feel unhappy; it was how you told your brain to *react* to this bad event or person. For instance, let's say two kids get dropped from the school tennis team. One kid cries for a week because she loves the game so much. The other is delighted, because now that she's not needed on the team she can spend Saturdays with her boyfriend! Now was being dropped from the tennis team bad or good? Neither. It all depends on our interpretations of the event, not the event itself.

So it is with nearly every area of life. We control our reality; our happiness or sadness is dependent on what we tell our minds. Never forget that. Once you truly understand it, you can transform your life. Where once you were just a puppet to your circumstances (feeling up when things were good and down when they were bad), now you can simply choose how you'll feel about things. If you experience a setback, you don't have to be miserable, because you can reprogram how you feel. Close your eyes and visualize. Program yourself to be happy in spite of the setback. How you feel is up to *you*!

Take control now by visualizing yourself being strong, powerful, and happy. Promise yourself that never again will you allow your circumstances to change your mood. From this moment on, when things get a little tough, use the awesome power of your brain to create the happier mood you want.

▼

MINUTE SEVEN:

Change Your Body Movements

▲

▶I want to tell you about some research that could revolutionize your life. It involves a relatively new but very exciting branch of human behavioral science known as Neuro-Linguistic Programming, or NLP for short.

The founders of NLP are two therapists, John Grinder and Richard Bandler, and they have been on the cutting edge of the human-potential movement for about the last twenty years. NLP is defined as the study of how language, both verbal and nonverbal, affects the nervous system. Don't be scared off by that technical talk; many aspects of NLP are both easy to understand and to apply. Yet the results of these simple actions can be absolutely astounding.

One of the most profound breakthroughs these NLP therapists have discovered involves the con-

Character is the basis of happiness
and happiness the sanction
of character.

—GEORGE SANTAYANA, philosopher

nection between body movement and human emotion.

Think about someone who's depressed. Isn't it often true that a sad person actually looks and moves like a sad person? A depressed person walks slowly, droops his or her shoulders, breathes more shallowly (occasionally letting out a long, sighing breath of exasperation), doesn't smile, and the eyes tend to look downward. Even a depressed person's voice is often different—slower, without vibrancy and power.

Isn't it also true that when we're happy our body movements are different? We move faster, smile more, talk more energetically, breathe more deeply, etc. . . . .

I think it's clear that our emotions change our physical movements. The breakthrough that the NLP people witnessed is that it works the other way around too! If you move as if you're happy, you actually begin to *become* happy.

It makes sense really. The brain, as we saw in "Minute 6," is a superpowerful computer. If you move a certain way when you're happy, your brain logically concludes you must be happy when you move like that! This is known as a cybernetic loop —happy thoughts create happy movements, and happy movements create happy thoughts.

Try it for yourself now. Sit down and simply put your body in the kind of position you would expect to be in if you were really depressed, as if you have been robbed for the thirtieth time this year and you have no insurance. Drop those shoulders, breathe weakly, put on a depressed face, even talk to yourself as though you're depressed. Go on, try doing this with 100-percent commitment for just one minute. Go!

> The world of the happy is quite
> another than the world of
> the unhappy.
>
> —LUDWIG WITTGENSTEIN, philosopher

How do you feel now? Not so good, huh? In just sixty measly seconds you began to feel a bit deflated, sadder, less vibrant. If you can begin to change your mood just by changing your posture in only one minute, imagine the effect slouching around the house in a depressed manner all day long has on your mood! And yet so many people spend *their whole lives* sitting around like this. These physical actions and postures are almost *guaranteeing* that these folks will feel lousy. They are constantly sending negative messages to their brain—hour after hour, day after day, year after year. Yuck.

Now try it the other way. Give this test complete

commitment, 100-percent effort. Sit in your seat as if you are absolutely ecstatic with joy. Put on a big smile, sit up, breathe deeply and relax, and put your body in the kind of position you'd be in if you felt absolutely fantastic, as if this is the happiest moment of your entire life. Relax in this euphoric, blissed-out state for one whole minute. Go for it!

How do you feel? If you've really put your effort into this exercise, you'll find your state has changed considerably. You'll be feeling much more relaxed, content, and happier than you were when you were in the depressed body position. This is because your body has sent a message to the brain via the nervous system that you're happy, and so your brain begins the necessary procedures to make you *feel* happy.

Remember, the subconscious mind is your servant, accepting whatever orders you give it. So start instructing your brain to feel good by acting as if you are feeling good.

Do you realize what a life-changing piece of information the body-mind cybernetic loop is? It means you never have to feel depressed for hours on end again! If you're feeling down, just start mov-

Aim for bliss. If you fail, you still
might hit happiness.

—JASPER ARGONOUS, philosopher

ing with absolute commitment to feeling happy and
your mood will soon pick up. This technique really
works, especially with practice. The difference it
can make to your mood is incredible. As the Neuro-
Linguistic Programmers put it, motion creates
emotion. (Actually, Doctors Grinder and Bandler
weren't the first to conceive this theory. No less a
figure than Charles Darwin suggested that we can
affect our emotions by our gestures and facial ex-
pressions in his book *The Expression of the Emotions in Man*. The year? 1872!)

Do you know how to stop crying? Smile, and
look up at something on the ceiling! It's almost impossible to cry when you do that. Why? Because
that body movement sends a different message to

> The essential tendency of life is toward happiness. . . . Optimism is the only true condition for a reasonable man.
>
> —PHILLIPS BROOKS, philanthropist

your brain! Imagine what an impact this can make on your life. If you're feeling tired from working late at the office, start moving around the office as if you're full of energy, and whammo! Your brain will give you the energy you need. If you're about to go on a big first date and you're feeling nervous because he/she/it is absolutely knockout gorgeous, just move around your home as if you're really relaxed and confident. If you walk and move as though you're confident, your brain gets the message to act that way. Want to feel sexy? *Move* sexily, and that's exactly how you'll begin to feel. You can be any way you want to be by changing your body movements and your thoughts, as they each depend on the other.

But you must, I repeat *must*, give it 100 percent. If you halfheartedly move about expecting to feel happy, it won't work. You've got to pretend you're on stage auditioning for a multimillion dollar movie deal, and it all depends on your acting brilliantly. When you go all out to act and move as if you're happy, your brain will immediately begin to give you the happier thoughts and feelings you desire.

▼

MINUTE EIGHT:

Change Your Focus

▲

Try this test; it's fascinating.

Look all around you and take note of everything that's blue in color. As you do, try to memorize the position each blue item is in. Stop reading and try it now. Once you feel satisfied that you're aware of the location of all the blue things, without looking around again try to remember where everything *red* is located. You can't, and the reason you're not able to is because of the brain's R.A.S.

Most people don't even know they have an R.A.S., and yet its job is incredibly important. R.A.S. stands for Reticular Activating System, and it's the part of the brain responsible for helping you focus.

Every human being is swamped by billions of pieces of data daily. Our eyes see millions of images; our noses detect thousands of smells; our ears pick up countless sounds. All this stimuli would com-

> Ultimately, the greatest service a
> woman can do her community is
> to be happy.
>
> —GERMAINE GREER, writer

pletely overwhelm us if the brain made us consciously aware of it all—in fact, it would drive us looney.

To save us from being taken away by the men in white coats, the brain's R.A.S. focuses only on what's important to us, and the irrelevant stuff never reaches our conscious minds. For instance, have you ever noticed that when you buy a new car you start seeing that brand of car everywhere? No, they didn't just start getting popular because you bought one; your brain's R.A.S. just starts picking up on those cars because that brand is now relevant to you.

What's all this got to do with getting happier? A

hell of a lot, actually. It's because of the R.A.S. that you must be careful what you focus on. For *what we focus on, we see.*

Just as if you focus on blue things you'll notice a lot of them, so too if you focus on what's bad in your life you will soon perceive your life as being mostly bad. If you take the position that your life is a disaster, you will notice a lot of evidence to prove yourself right; but likewise, if you take the stance that your life is great, you'll find a lot of proof for that line of thought.

So many of us allow ourselves to think any old thought, even if it's worthless, unconstructive, and negative. As a result of not guiding the thoughts we focus on, we become the slaves of circumstances, rather than their master.

This is no way to live, and it's certainly no recipe for lasting happiness. If we are to have even a chance of being happy, we must discipline ourselves to focus on the good in all events, no matter how bad the events may at first appear.

Truly powerful and successful people have the ability to control their focus. When everyone around them sees failure, they choose to see possibility. A

The two foes of human happiness
are pain and boredom.

—ARTHUR SCHOPENHAUER, philosopher

classic example is Thomas Edison, perhaps the greatest inventor who ever graced this planet. Apparently Edison tried more than 10,000 separate experiments before he successfully created a rudimentary electric light. According to folklore, an assistant came to him one day after he'd experienced his latest failure and asked him this poignant question: "Mr. Edison, do you think you'll fail 10,000 times to create an electric light?" Edison looked him squarely in the eye and replied, "I haven't failed nearly 10,000 times to invent the electric light. I've discovered over 9,000 ways *not* to invent it!"

To Edison, each failure was a success, because it meant one less stone he had to unturn. His whole outlook was different from that of the average person. By choosing to focus on the good, he was able to enjoy his work and therefore his life much more.

Helen Keller is another paragon of possibility thinking. If you became blind and deaf, you might have every right to be utterly miserable. Not Helen Keller. She not only mastered language and educated herself, but she educated millions of others in the appreciation of life by her extraordinary words and deeds too. Clearly she was someone who thought differently from the average person. She once wrote: "When one door closes, another one always opens. But so many people only see the closed door, they fail to see the potential opportunities the newly opened door brings."

Or in other words—control your focus and you'll be happier. Choose to look for the good in every situation and your life will be full of good. Is it naive to assume that there is good in everything bad that happens to us? Am I suffering from a severe case of Pollyanna Syndrome?

Bob Proctor wouldn't think so. Proctor is one of Canada's greatest human-potential consultants, and his knowledge of the human mind is awesome. Proctor advocates a theory known as the Law of

> Happiness makes up in height for
> what it lacks in length.
>
> —ROBERT FROST, poet

Polarity. Simply stated, the Law of Polarity says that everything has an opposite. There can be no light if there isn't darkness, no sound if there isn't silence, no heat if there isn't cold. As applied to our daily lives, there can be no bad event without some good coming from it. The trick is to find that good and focus on it, thereby improving your mood.

This theory has a lot of merit to it, in my experience. Truly, no matter how disastrous a situation, there is always much good that comes out of it. Let's pick an extreme hypothetical example to really test the theory.

Pretend that your house has been robbed. "What's good about that?" you ask. Well, for one thing, for the rest of your life I bet you'll make sure your house is highly secured, with a burglar alarm, locks on all windows, and maybe even a dog as well. You've just ensured that for the rest of your life your possessions are likely to be safer—you might never have done that if your house had not been robbed. (You'll also have a lot of fun frolicking with the dog that you wouldn't have had otherwise.) The robbery will also teach you some good lessons as well—not to take your possessions for granted; to value your family (after all, if they had been at home, something terrible might have happened); to support the police; to not waste hard-earned money on ridiculously expensive jewelry that might get stolen the very next week. As a result of the burglary, you might elect to learn self-defense. If you did, it would lead to better health and a considerable improvement in self-esteem.

The fact that you've been robbed opens up some exciting possibilities as well. For example, let's assume they took all your clothes. With the insurance money you'd have the chance to buy a whole new wardrobe. (You certainly wouldn't have done that if you hadn't been robbed.) If they took your TV, that's surely an opportunity to buy the state-of-the-art one you've been drooling over down at the mall.

No doubt you'll tell all your friends about the burglary. Isn't it likely that a few of them might tighten up their home security upon hearing of your unfortunate experience? These security measures may well save your friends from being robbed too, which is surely a good thing.

And so it goes on. If you really thought about it, I suspect you could find a very long list of good things that would result directly from the apparent catastrophe of being robbed. The same goes for virtually any piece of bad luck you may experience.

Better by far you should
forget and smile
Than that you should
remember and be sad.

—CHRISTINA ROSSETTI, poet

The key is to look for the good in every situation and focus on it. Then your happiness is sure to increase. Whenever something disastrous, irritating, or just plain nauseating happens, train yourself to ask this simple question:

What's good about this?

Really think about the answers, and when you've got a list, then focus your thoughts on those good things. The more you focus on the good in the situation, the more the pain will disappear. Focus on the negative part of the experience, and the pain will increase. It's entirely up to you.

That's the question you ask yourself if you're unhappy because of a particular event. But what about if you're just generally down in the dumps for no reason at all? Haven't you had days when you just woke up feeling lousy, and stayed that way all day? I know I have. In fact this unexplained lethargy really got my curiosity up, so I decided to check out what the scientists said about it.

I came up with two answers, one easy to understand and one a bit more radical. I'll give you the simple one first.

Physiologists believe that often you're feeling

I count myself in nothing
else so happy
As in a soul remembering
my friends.

—WILLIAM SHAKESPEARE, poet-playwright

down in the morning because of what you ate (and indeed how you ate) the night before. If you consume a huge meal with lots of meat just before bedtime, you virtually guarantee lethargy upon awakening. The simple reason is that your mind may have been sleeping but your body has been working full steam trying to digest all that heavy stuff. If you want to avoid that early morning sluggish feeling in mind and body:

1. Finish your meal at least two hours before hitting the sack.
2. Don't eat a whole lot of meat for dinner.

Dinner should be the lightest meal of the day, because the physical activity following dinner usually does not require much food energy. (Okay, you midnight sex maniacs can eat a bit more.)

If diet is the conservative explanation for morning unhappiness, then what's the radical one?

Well, many dream psychologists believe that if you have a stressful, exhausting, frightening, or depressing dream, then you're much more likely to be tired and irritable in the morning. After all, when you're dreaming your subconscious doesn't know that you're dreaming. It responds to that six-headed 300-foot-high kangaroo bouncing toward you as though it's absolutely real! So you're totally involved in your dream, and all that running, screaming, fighting, and crying exhausts the mind. Likewise, if you have a massively depressing dream, does it not make sense that some trace of those emotions may remain in your mind when you awake? It's definitely an interesting theory, at least.

Whether you're depressed when you wake up or unhappy at any other time of the day, there's an extremely effective technique you can use to help you get you out of the rut, and feeling happier fast.

> Happiness seems made to
> be shared.
>
> —PIERRE CORNEILLE, playwright

Remembering that your emotional state is usually due to what you are focusing on, when you're feeling down ask yourself this simple question:

What can I be happy about in my life?

Then really focus on those things. You may like to list the people who care for you. List your particular talents; everybody has something they're good at. Everybody. What about the things you have already achieved? Think hard enough and you'll find a whole stack of good things you've accomplished. Do you have eyesight? Well, that's something to be deliriously happy about and grateful for. Do you have two legs? There are millions in the world who'd give up virtually everything to have two legs. Do you have a job? You might not like it that much, but there are at least a hundred million people in the world who would consider being employed a dream come true. Do you have a place to sleep at night? You may want to add a swimming pool or renovate the bathroom, but again, millions of people don't even have a roof to sleep under.

My favorite source of reasons to be happy is Barbara Ann Kipfer's joyous book, *14,000 Things To Be Happy About.* In it she lists scores of things you and I may take for granted but which also cause at least a little bit of happiness. She reminds us to be happy about:

- a lake catching the last flecks of sunlight coming in over the pines
- fresh ginger muffins
- funny toes
- a cathedral of trees
- crisp cotton dresses
- sexy music
- dairy cows
- sunflowers
- mattresses
- margaritas
- brake fluid
- warm sun and seaspray

The happiest moments of my life
have been the few which I have
passed at home in the bosom of
my family.

—THOMAS JEFFERSON, statesman-
philosopher

And about 13,990 more things . . .

Take a minute to make your own happiness list
now in the space provided.

I'm Happy About:

1. _____

2. _____

3. _____

4. _____

5. _____

6. _____

7. _____

8. _____

9. _____

10. _____

11. _____

12. _____

13. _____

14. _____

15. _____

16. _____

17. _____

18. _____

19. _____

20. _____

Looking at the list you've made, don't you feel that life's really not so bad? Unless we remind ourselves of all the good things, we are sure to dwell on the bad. And that's the extraordinary value of "Minute Eight" of the mood-changing process.

It's all a matter of getting things in perspective, isn't it? Consider this for a moment. The legendary scientist Carl Sagan estimates that there may well be over one hundred billion planets in our galaxy alone. If that's so, how big could any of the Earth's problems be in the grand scheme of things? How tiny must our own individual problems be? Sure, we think they're big because we're involved with them, but in the big picture, the Earth is like a speck of sand on a million-mile beach. Don't you think it's about time we stopped taking our lives so seriously? One of the powerful benefits of the "Minute Eight" questions is that they force you to balance your perspective, to see more of the big picture instead of obsessing over your own little world.

If, whenever you're down, you continually ask yourself "What's good about this?" and "What can I be happy about in my life?" it will totally alter the

> This is the true joy of life, the
> being used for a purpose
> recognized by yourself as a mighty
> one; . . . instead of [being] a
> feverish selfish little clod of
> ailments and grievances
> complaining that the world will not
> devote itself to making you happy.
>
> —GEORGE BERNARD SHAW, playwright

way you view your problems. Remember that for every bad event, there's always a good opportunity. The Law of Polarity is immutable.

When you train yourself to think of twenty good things for every bad thing in your life, how could you possibly feel miserable? Those good things exist, they really do; we just have to discipline ourselves to remember them. By regularly asking your-

self "What's good about this?" and "What can I be
happy about in my life?" your perceptions of your
situation *must* change for the better. For when it
comes to your conscious mind and your moods, per-
ception really is reality.

Living a Life
Filled with
Happiness

Congratulations! You now possess the tools to become happy in eight minutes!

In case your memory's as bad as mine, let's review this unique happiness system, step by step:

Step One is to *stimulate the thymus gland* by smiling, tapping the thymus, and placing your tongue in the centering position. Be sure to make it a big, wide, crow's-feet-creating smile.

Step Two is to *change your breathing*, utilizing much more of your lung capacity.

Step Three is to *drink fruit juice* to allow the powerful compound glucose to temporarily improve how you're feeling.

Step Four is *visualization* to change how you see yourself.

Step Five is to *move your body as though you're already happy*, with total commitment.

> Happiness is produced not so much by great pieces of good fortune that seldom happen as by little advantages that occur every day.
>
> —BENJAMIN FRANKLIN, statesman-philosopher

Finally, Step Six is to *change the focus of your thoughts*, concentrating on all the good elements in your life.

If you do these techniques properly, it is physiologically impossible not to improve your mood. They are based on decades of research on how the brain works. They'll work for the young and they'll work for the old. You are never more than eight minutes away from happiness.

Isn't that a delightful thought?

Commit this process to memory, and then

take the opportunity to use it when life gets a bit rough—or whenever you want to convert feeling just okay into feeling great. Remember that your ability to alter your moods can't be super powerful unless you practice the techniques regularly. Even if you don't have any fruit juice around, or if you only have a few moments to spare, take time to do at least a couple of the techniques. They all work individually to alter your state, but in combination they can revolutionize how you feel.

After a period of learning, you'll find yourself making stunning progress in empowering your mind. Pretty soon your powers of visualization will become so strong that you'll want to use your "movie mind" to get other things in life besides a better mood. For example, regularly visualize yourself performing well at work. As sure as night follows day, you will begin to perform better. To sceptics this seems crazy, but it is only ignorance of the brain's mechanisms that creates the doubt. Once you truly understand how that thing between your ears works, you'll not only believe in spectacular abilities; you'll expect them.

Share the secrets of mood changing with your

> Mankind are always happy for having been happy, so that if you make them happy now, you make them happy twenty years hence by the memory of it.
>
> —SYDNEY SMITH, writer

loved ones, and your life will be even more transformed. Imagine if all your close friends and family were more happy more often. The quality of all of your lives would increase immeasurably.

Always remember that your performance is a result of the state you're in. If you can get yourself to feel happy and powerful virtually all the time, then you're far more likely to succeed in whatever you wish to do. Don't be like the millions of people who mope around depressed, slowly planting the seeds of illness in their bodies. Know that as you get yourself into a great mood, you are revitalizing your

> Happiness does not depend on outward things, but on the way we see them.
>
> —LEO TOLSTOY, writer

body and massively increasing your chances of living longer. For as we saw in Chapter One, it is a proven fact that happiness helps create health, and vice versa.

Now that you've learned how to get your mind in a happier mood, what about a more lasting happiness? That's a harder question.

Why are so many people miserable—even the ones who have all the yachts, fame, houses, lovers, and Gucci loafers they could ever want? At the same time, why are there people who have little but a body and a loincloth who are blissfully happy? Of course, this question has plagued, intrigued, and captivated mankind since Gronk the Caveman was a youngster, and in a book of this brevity I can hardly pretend to offer a definitive answer. But I can let you know what researchers who have spent decades investigating happiness have found.

First, we must look at the work of Mihaly Csikszentmihalyi and David Myers. Mihaly is a pioneer in the field of "bliss research" and is also the author of the deeply illuminating book, *The Psychology of Optimal Experience* (later reprinted under the more user-friendly title of *The Psychology Of Happiness*).

This eminent University of Chicago professor did in-depth interviews with people of all ages, many walks of life, and many cultures. He found that those who enjoyed life most were those who tended to immerse themselves in "flow" activities. What is a flow activity? It's one that totally involves you, that really uses your skills. It is the midpoint between anxiety and boredom, that place where you are deeply challenged, yet are totally in control. It can be writing, skiing, cooking, driving—anything! You forget time, you lose yourself in the task, you're clear on the goal, and you're making progress toward it. According to Professor Csikszentmihalyi, the more you can fill your life with such flow activities (at work and at play) the happier you will be.

The social researcher David Myers, who summarized his findings on happiness in the very accessible book *The Pursuit of Happiness*, believes that there are four character traits that people who are happy tend to have.

The first characteristic Myers credits with helping psychological well-being is self-esteem. Happy people like themselves. The second is personal control. Happy people believe they are running their own ship, not merely following orders in life. Third, he cites plain old optimism—happy people are full of hope. Finally, and somewhat curiously, his research indicates that simple extroversion helps you

Happiness is not an ideal of reason but of imagination.

—IMMANUEL KANT, philosopher

enjoy life. Happy people tend to be more outgoing.

Of course, some people may be lucky enough to be born with these happiness-inducing characteristics, but the rest of us should not lose hope. Any character trait you wish to have can be developed. It may take some will power, persistence, and time, but it most certainly can be done. Examples of shy people becoming confident, pessimistic people becoming optimistic, and people with low self-esteem developing a strong self-image are numerous in the annals of psychology. You can do it, if you really want to and you're prepared to work at it.

As for my own research, I have observed that people I know to be deeply happy all share the following lifestyle components:

Happy people have energy.

I do not know a single soul who claims to be happy who is weak of mind or body. Happy people exude energy, real verve, and get-up-and-go. A lot of this energy no doubt comes from having lives that include meaningful goals and dreams, projects and ideas that really inspire them to get out of bed each morning. But a lot of their power clearly also comes from having a healthy, active lifestyle. I sim-

> The world is so full of a
> number of things,
> I'm sure we should all be
> as happy as kings.
>
> —ROBERT LOUIS STEVENSON, writer

ply do not believe that you can be blissful in the long term without taking the time to replenish and build your body's energy reserves.

Exercise doesn't have to be vigorous, but it does have to be regular. A walk with the dog each evening can do wonders. Even daily deep breathing exercises are enough to make a big impact on energy levels over time. But without some kind of energetic activity, your body becomes fragile and your brain dulled.

Happy people are giving.

Those who are truly happy are more than just prepared to give to others; they positively delight

> The chief happiness for a man is
> to be what he is.
>
> —ERASMUS, philosopher

in giving. It seems to me that the most selfish people I know are also among the unhappiest. Selfish people invariably have a scarcity mentality, believing that giving to others means that they will have less in their own life. This thinking ignores one of the most basic laws of nature: "For every action there is an equal and opposite reaction." If you give something away, it is an inviolable natural law that you will get its equivalent back somewhere, sometime, and in some form.

Furthermore, it may also increase your longevity. During the eighties a major study was done in China on people who were over one hundred years old. One of the lifestyle traits virtually all of these centenarians had was that they liked to help other people, either through their choice of work or in their personal lives.

Happy people have balanced lifestyles.

The quickest route to misery is to become obsessed with one aspect of your life. If all you're concerned about is business, then your family life is going to suffer. If all you're interested in is hitting the discos and partying all night long, then your health is going to suffer eventually. If all you want is to be super fit and you spend your life exercising, then don't expect to be rich.

Living a life obsessed with one thing can be exciting and even rewarding in the short term, but unless you at least take care of the other areas, it will ultimately leave you feeling empty inside. I'm not suggesting you become a "jack of all trades and master of none"; if you love doing something then pursue it with passion, but don't make your life unbalanced while you're doing it.

Happy people refuse to neglect any part of their life. They nurture all areas: physical, mental, spiritual, financial, social, and family. They may focus on one, but not to the total detriment of the others.

Happy people also balance the *pace* of their

> Happiness is the only sanction of
> life; where happiness fails,
> existence remains a mad and
> lamentable experiment.
>
> —GEORGE SANTAYANA, philosopher

lives. A life that's always Go! Go! Go! may sound glamorous, but in reality after a while it overtaxes the mind and depletes the body. For all the hysterical times, there must be quiet times to allow the system to recuperate. Actually, if you want a good model for living in a balanced way, look no further than Mother Nature herself.

For instance, watch an animal's behavior. Animals don't get frustrated and think negative thoughts all day. When a stressful situation arises they deal with it efficiently and then slip back into a relaxed mode within minutes. We can learn a lot from them. Here's another example: plants don't try to flower all year long. They know there's a time for flowering, a time for resting, and a time for building up their energies to flower again. Workaholics could pick up a tip or two from them.

The more you watch the cycles of nature, the more you realize that she has worked out the best ways to handle virtually any scenario. In fact, there's an ancient school of Asian philosophy based on following nature; it's known as Taoism, after "Tao," which means "the way." By observing nature at work and applying its principles, the Taoists were able to improve their lives, their health, their scientific knowledge, and their luck.

For example, the Taoists noted that when tree branches were alive, they were flexible, and when they were stiff, it usually meant the tree was dead. Likewise, when a person's body is flexible she's alive, and when it's completely hard she too is dead. From this they concluded that one must maintain flexibility if one wants a long and healthy life. Flexibility in body, in mind, in business plans, and in personal relationships.

Every time I talk to a savant I feel quite sure that happiness is no longer a possibility. Yet when I talk with my gardener, I'm convinced of the opposite.

—BERTRAND RUSSELL, philosopher (ATTRIB.)

Happy people seem to have this flexibility in their lives. If things don't go their way they work around the problem, rather than getting upset and stressed about it. Of course, you don't have to be a Taoist or a nature lover to have a happy life, but certainly most happy people seem to have the sense of *balance* in their lives that nature exhibits.

Happy people believe in themselves.

The power of belief on the human body and mind is awesome. In 1920 Dr. Emil Coué reported over five times the average success rate in curing

> Happiness is a warm puppy.
>
> —CHARLES M. SCHULTZ, _Peanuts_ creator

patients by simply changing their beliefs. His main method? Getting them to say often "Every day in every way I am getting better and better." Incredibly, that was enough to gradually change their beliefs, which in turn slowly changed their physical condition.

Once, running a mile in under four minutes was considered physically impossible. Physicians would swear that the human body could not move at that speed, and everybody believed them. Well, almost everybody.

A young athlete named Roger Bannister deeply believed in his own abilities, and sure enough, after years of heartbreaking effort, in 1954 Bannister ran the mile in under four minutes. Then, something else incredible happened. The next year _twelve_

▼

A modern "happy home recipe" includes: 4 cups of love, 2 cups of loyalty, 3 cups of forgiveness, 1 cup of friendship, 5 spoons of hope, 2 spoons of tenderness, 4 quarts of faith, 1 barrel of laughter. Take love and loyalty, mix thoroughly with faith. Blend it with tenderness, kindness, and understanding. Add friendship and hope, sprinkle abundantly with laughter. Bake it with sunshine. Serve daily with generous helpings.

—ANONYMOUS

▲

athletes broke the four-minute mark. Twelve! Although just one year before it was believed to be impossible. And the year after that, over *two hundred* people ran the mile in under four minutes.

So what happened? Did all these athletes dramatically change their training habits? Did they all go on a strict diet of bananas or something? Of course not. The only things these athletes changed were their beliefs, but that was enough to transform them. Changing your beliefs can transform you too.

Happy people have different beliefs from other people. They tend to believe that they're good enough to lick their problems, no matter how tough they may be. They have faith in themselves, in their abilities and their dreams. They also believe that life is really worth living, and importantly, they believe that happiness is achievable.

Are they right or are they just kidding themselves? It doesn't matter. As Henry Ford once said, "Whether you think you can or you can't, you're right." The belief creates the reality. Belief is a choice. If you truly seek happiness, you must choose to believe in yourself, and believe happiness is possible. Unless you foster that belief in yourself, your happiness will evaporate the moment things get a little hard.

We become what we focus on, so you've got to decide to focus on becoming happy. Get up in the morning, look in the mirror, and say "Today is going to be one of the happiest days of the year." Then commit to making that affirmation a reality. The more you focus on achieving happiness, the more you'll realize that happines has very little to do with what happens to you that day. What really matters is your reaction to those events.

You can either laugh it off or take the whole world on your shoulders; it's entirely up to you. As Shakespeare wrote, "Nothing is good or bad, but thinking makes it so." But one way of thinking leads to a life of bitterness and angst, and the other to a life of smiles and joy.

We tend to get so obsessed with getting things that we forget why we're chasing after all the cars, clothes, and houses in the first place. Of course, we're trying to feel happier. But why would you pursue some material goal for years to feel happy, when you can get yourself in a happy state in eight minutes? Beats me.

True happiness will permeate your life when you realize that the greatest fountain of joy comes from inside of you. When you discover who you truly are. When you discover that human beings don't need external things to make themselves happy; it all comes from within. Promise yourself that you'll use the techniques in this book starting today. Never again let your circumstances create your mood, and never again accept being any way but happy. You'll be amazed at the effect a dedication to happiness will have on your life.

Have a happy day.

> A man is happy so long as he chooses to be happy and nothing can stop him.
>
> —ALEXANDER SOLZHENITSYN, writer

The Happiness
Library

I enjoy studying the art and science of happiness. Many of my spare hours are spent perusing books from all over the world on this subject, from the ancient to the modern. Truly, some of my best friends are these books. They are a constant source of delight, of wonder, of guidance and wisdom. Like good friends, some of them are harder to find than others.

To be honest, building up my happiness library has been a long, arduous task. For every book that opened my mind, there were ten that put me to sleep. Time and time again I'd purchase a book only to set it down on the coffee table an hour later, disappointed. To save you the ten years of searching I had to go through to build a great happiness library, in this last chapter I'm going to tell you about a few of the books that have changed my life.

———

> If one thinks that one is happy,
> that is enough to be happy.
>
> —MADAME DE LA FAYETTE, writer

Some of these books are about material happiness, how to get all the stuff you've always dreamed of having. Some are more concerned with spiritual happiness, peeling back the layers of our very existence. All of them are powerful. Each one has the potential to change your life in very meaningful ways.

Here's my list of all-time "hits," categorized under Success, Health, and Spiritual Happiness.

Success and Happiness

As a Man Thinketh by James Allen

First published in 1910 and reprinted ever since, this book gets to the very heart of what creates

> To fill the hour—that is happiness;
> to fill the hour, and leave no
> crevice for a repentance or
> an approval.
>
> —RALPH WALDO EMERSON, writer-
> philosopher

success and happiness in life: thought. That's what every page of this book is about—how even your teeny-weeniest thoughts create your future life. After reading this book, you will truly understand how you got to wherever you are in life, and how everything that happens to you is in your power.

Think and Grow Rich by Napoleon Hill

A classic in the field. Few books have made more millionaires than this one. I first read it when I was seventeen and it was instrumental in molding my mind for financial success. The author spent

> All who joy would win
> Must share it—Happiness
> was born a twin.
>
> —LORD BYRON, poet

over 20 years interviewing the richest and most successful men in America before he began writing this book. How's that for commitment! His dedication shows in the wisdom that's on every page.

Tactics by Edward de Bono

Edward de Bono invented the concept of Lateral Thinking, and he lectures around the world on how to be creative. But my favorite of his books is not about creativity but about success. *Tactics* is an indepth study of fifty or so of the world's most successful sports people, business persons, and artists of modern times. It is highly revealing. It would be difficult *not* to find financial happiness after putting this book's lessons into practice.

How to Be Rich by John Paul Getty

If Getty didn't know how to get rich then who does? One of America's first billionaires, Getty wrote a "warts and all" exposé of the necessary steps to massive wealth. He discussed the traditional wealth sources—real estate, oil, stocks—in a lively and entertaining way. Particularly helpful is Getty's advice to the young on their way up the ladder.

Health and Happiness

The Complete Book of Chinese Health and Healing: Guarding the Three Treasures by Daniel Reid

This is the most outstanding health book I have read in the last decade. Reid, a Taoist doctor and scholar, combines ancient healing systems and cutting-edge western medicine with ease. The three treasures are Ching, basic fluids of the human body like blood, lymph, and sexual essence; Chi, the basic

> That all who are happy, are equally
> happy, is not true. Happiness
> consists in the multiplicity of
> agreeable consciousness.
>
> —SAMUEL JOHNSON, writer

energy of the body; and Shen, or spirit, which is the mind and all its workings.

In simple language, the author proves that there is a lot more to being healthy than most of us realize. Buy it for everyone you care about.

The Art of Chi Kung by Wong K. Kit

This takes Reid's concept of Chi much further. You may not have heard of the mysterious stuff in your body called Chi, but believe me, you'll be learning a lot more about it soon. Now that China is opening up to the West, its ancient medical secrets are being unveiled, and the concept of Chi is

Ask yourself whether you are
happy, and you cease to be so.

—JOHN STUART MILL, philosopher

at the very heart of Chinese medicine. This book
clearly shows you what Chi does in your body and
how, with the right Chi exercises, you can build
your health and emotional happiness up to staggering strength.

Dr. Kenneth Cooper's Antioxidant Revolution by Dr. Kenneth Cooper

Chi and antioxidants, that's where I believe the
physical happiness breakthroughs will be in the
next century. Written by the popular and insightful
inventor of aerobics, Dr. Kenneth Cooper, this book
explains what antioxidants are and how they can
keep us healthy and happy long into our twilight
years.

Perfect Health by Deepak Chopra

Chopra is the reigning king of mind-body medicine, and a delightful writer to boot. *Perfect Health* was one of his first books and is certainly one of his finest. In it Deepak reveals a wonderfully effective Indian system of medicine called Ayurveda. Ayurvedic medicine is very natural, very easy to do, and extremely effective. It would be impossible to follow Chopra's Ayurvedic lifestyle and not become healthier and happier.

Spiritual Happiness

There is such a treasure trove of material in this area that it is very difficult for me to pick my all-time favorites. However, each of the books listed below has changed me profoundly for the better.

Autobiography of a Yogi by Paramahansa Yogananda

What a classic this is! It really is one of the great modern spiritual adventure stories, a magic carpet ride through the higher realms of consciousness. The book takes us through Yogananda's growth

> I have learned, in whatsoever state
> I am, therewith to be content.
>
> —SAINT PAUL

from a precocious child just discovering his innate powers to his current role as majestic spiritual leader of thousands.

Yogananda shows us the strong link between Christianity and Hinduism, the amazing paranormal abilities lying hidden in mankind, and the joy of exploring the spiritual wonderland that is India.

The Sufi Way to Happiness
by Shaykh Fadhlalla Haeri

The Sufis are Islamic mystics, masters of meditation living in the world but totally devoted to God. They are said to possess miraculous powers, like telepathy, clairvoyance, and the ability to travel astrally. Whether you believe that or not doesn't mat-

> Wisdom is the supreme part
> of happiness.
>
> —SOPHOCLES, playwright

ter; the book has enough down-to-earth information on how to live a happier life to make reading it worthwhile. If you can't locate this particular book, settle for any book on Sufism—you will be rewarded with a most useful philosophy of life, love, happiness, and success.

Tao-te Ching by Lao-tzu

This book has been translated more times by scholars than any other book in the world, other than the Bible. Words can't describe its value—just read with an open mind and see for yourself.

Remember this, that very little is needed to make a happy life.

—MARCUS AURELIUS, statesman-philosopher

Other Recommended Books for Your Happiness Library

Make the Most of Your Mind by Tony Buzan

Flow: The Psychology of Optimal Experience by Mihalyi Csikszentmihaly

Wake Up Your Creative Genius by Kurt Hanks and J. A. Parry

Light on Yoga by B. K. Iyengar

14,000 Things to Be Happy About by Barbara Ann Kipfer

The Pursuit of Happiness by David Myers

Awaken the Giant Within by Anthony Robbins

Learned Optimism by Dr. Martin Seligman

> Well, I've had a happy life.
>
> —WILLIAM HAZLITT, writer (last words)